SHAKE A SPEAR
WITH ME,
JOHN BERRYMAN

new poems and a play

by

Edwin Honig

shake a spear with me,
john berryman

COPPER BEECH PRESS

The author wishes to thank the editors and publishers
in which some of these poems first appeared: *Boston
University Journal,* for "Lines for Dancers"; *New
York Quarterly,* for "His Chain," "His Dream," "His
Song," "After Eurydice," "After Orpheus," "Another
Orpheus"; *New Directions in Prose and Poetry 24,*
for "Orpheus Below."

Copper Beech Press

Box 1852

Brown University

Providence, Rhode Island 02912

for Sophie Hawkes and Jack

CONTENTS

Shake a Spear With Me, John Berryman

Another Orpheus

SHAKE A SPEAR WITH ME, JOHN BERRYMAN

She's Yours

Take and button her in
She lies outside waiting
A sort of something
On your mind
Pretending you have
Nothing for her

You die to see her straight
But she is always out there
Lingering sideways
About to go
And as she turns to leave
Trembling to be taken in

Lullaby

The eyes you dim for her
Are in her care
She sees with them
As she brightens
Steps out clear
You almost aren't there

You have one hand
She made two
Out of the enemy other
Arms and shoulders
Went with them
Now you don't need any

Without her you're lame
With her about the same
Ask it and she drops everything
To bring you off
Even curtains the blinking mind
Your star blind basket

Shadow Me You

What hunger hunted for is plain
A sucked out box of aftertaste
Grave of self unselfed
A tongueless mouth
A skull unbrained
Soon to be inhabited
Membered to again what
In the end it would let out
And have to do without

Who says all this
Some What
Possibly
An It
That afterward
Is me
Your me
Chucked into
My brain

Ill Be Well

Grave doubts sacked
The poisoned he
Staggering around that
Maimed mass of you
Ready to cave in
When you gave out
You did him in

Did he slip you or you him
Who wants to know
All knowing is decline
I read you here where
Now is equilibrium
With me flipped out
You kicking still

What's True

Rings round here sometimes landing
All light dark before it falls

Is that what turns the wind
The wind asks who asks the same

The same is oneness' twin
Failing itself to fall

Self remains as light remains
A washed out gall

Seesaw Songs

Poor I came alone
you said
into a world
without me

> *Pure I came with*
> *nothing coupled yet*
> *When I thought*
> *mind married world*

You spoke
I have a mind
no space holds
I soar where
nothing lands
or was before

> As you spoke
> space held
> your mind
> slipped between
> its jaws
> This was all before

Mind squared the world
Angles rebounded it
Light became
a fool's gold then

        Alighting then it saw
        only as sight itself sees
        pureness hovering
        on mouldy gall

Out of darkness then
it came alone
older than darkness
that spread mould

        Light launched itself
        in us till all
        that we became
        we saw

THROUGH YOU

Glass I've wanted to live
through you
to be returned to me so

I'd drink the light I see
where you live
in a time you'll always be

without knowing I am
watching me
appear there in you when

wishing not to be ends
with your silent
Now walk through me

LINES FOR DANCERS

Dolls remember
waiting to be born

an empty turmoil
in the head

the memory
of milk

a quiet shifting
in the straw

*

The body straight
the body folded
then poise
altering the center
the difficult
destruction
of a thoughtless
balance

*

The sexual body
dropping
in a chair
in bed

under him
on her

down

and the neutral
wisdom
to rise
again

from broken
stances

up

*

Gesture after gesture
sometimes hardens them

the music stops
but nothing can slacken them

curled up on their sides
night and day

bodies dance to reproduce themselves
with all their might

and faces lock desperate
to be always blank

WHO

It is your last day and hour and you are alone
No one is coming but that thing
You have nothing to say even to yourself
Your mind is almost blank
A fly is buzzing in the room
    You can kill the fly but you don't   Your thoughts
begin but they are not on the fly   They are without color
without depth   They skim across your mind   Before you can
read them they disappear
    Now after ten minutes or thirty you begin to hear
words spoken words
    You think   Who speaks   You are greedy for a human
sound a presence
    Who speaks   Who is speaking
    It is a half-friendly Who like your mother when you were
a child   Soft encouraging voice with the querulous edge
    The words fade   The voice fades going over the edge
over a waterfall and disappears
    You look around the room   It is bare yet things are in
it with names your mind will not name
    You look around the room turning your neck twisting
your shoulder

You stoop you kneel you lie down
You get up quickly
There is the voice with the words again
Who you ask
Be still it says
Who
Be still

A silence grows till words start again   a voice slowly speaking as you listen quickening with words speaking faster more lively

Who
You think it is like your father
No
It is like
No
Yourself
Yes

It is coming faster   the room is turning   you are on your knees again weeping   the ceiling moves down

Words pour out of you faster clearer fresher full of feeling never before spoken words never heard before   gushing out of you

You they say you they say you they say you

You Youyou Youyouyouyou Breaking out of your chest surging out till you join them and you are all of them at once a long water flowing a long stream widening flooding an ocean sea world all water without earth or sky a water all water over forever

ANOTHER ORPHEUS

His Chain

How he had made
link after link
his mind to her heart
thinking loosely to join
not to imprison
each to its self
and worlds apart
then when it jarred
he suddenly turned

His Dream

How he had sat
huddled all night
failed faces passing
the narrowing light
the windswept street
watching the fire
die in its ashes

How from the ashes
he learned of root forces
the powerful hand
that would crack
the light open
the day he must break
to be born

Another

within this leaf
a life
within this life
a soul
with messages
trees hear
inhere
as we who are
cohere
in what we see

while
toward
this tree
this leaf
we
only
may appear
to be
and bear
apart

A Wind Dies

A wind lies down
Nothing in the tree
but frozen space
between the leaves

No sound
but underneath
the tree a shadow
strains to feel
the tree is moving
wind in the leaves
still passing

A wind has died forever
A tree forever frozen
deepening a shadow
tears itself to pieces

His Song

Speaking in time
of the slow removal
of parts
the whole unspoken
unseen

slide-back surmounting
slide-forward
and upward beyond us
no further
than where

everywhere centered
is folded
into the down-plunging
circle
working within

who-we-will-be moving
within us without us
till brushing each
meets ourselves
in the other

moving us toward
each outward one
who is the other
brushing each
into us past

The Silence

Something long past just heard us
and I think whatever it was
heard us before

Because as we changed it changed
as we passed it passed
fading behind us

All it wanted was to be with us
partaking of all
we enjoyed

And suffering when we were
but only to make us aware
we had its support

*How many coffins have failed
to contain their contents*
it would observe

Or if too wrapped up in each other
would sigh *Wonders assail me
I cannot keep up*

When we thought we could speak
without marring our own
silent rapport

We asked what in the world
we had brought on ourselves
just by being alone

Maybe we'd both grown numb
to the feeling of being
alone together

On some pretext we parted
wanting the chance of being
untogether alone

But remember how sick of the ruse
we got until we just
had to make up

And coming back made us
too happy to think at all
Thinking spoils things

Then you noticed we hadn't been feeling
the steady old drain
the presence or loss

The dark was all solid darkness
a day so many hours of light
No strange touch or word

So that now when you turned you thought
whatever's outside the window
is surely a bird

Whether outside or inside
it surely is listening
and gratefully heard

Her Remoteness

We sat in the lamplight's quiet estimation
of our wavering unanswered fire, one moment
in our living brimful glass
containing each of us, each as yet untouched,
unbroken, asking, Who
will drink us if we do not drink each other?
And neither of us stirred.

*

It is a light lingering on a sill
as I lie half-wakened on a summer morning
sunk in the weighted gladness
of my beached body still awash and unreleased
by the dark tide of sleep
till I advance a hand to touch the light and it
withdraws however far I reach and disappears.

After Eurydice

That all may be heard
at love's dying
sounds leap from his mouth
a nightmare unburdens
joy's separation
releases a body
watching amazed

Anguish returning
earth's presence
worming it-may-be
into it-will-be
thought seeds shoot out
of the powerful tree
her cold glinting absence

Words found for no words
sprout from his mouth
lips and tongue
toe touch and glances
move into being
animal bodies
waking to praise

Melting Song

Fire be Water

Hear Fire reply

I am Water already
all things you dream of you see
rainfall the tree
perfect limbs drowning
me they become that am you
drifting a breath
burning to Earth

Cried the Earth
cried the Air

Water be Fire

And Water
silently nodded
I am

After Orpheus

Blame me
his heart
a wounded dog
trapped in the woods
returns

sits after years
on the bare floor
so still
unbreathing head low
almost stone

Blame me
turns slowly
fire leaps higher
birds fall grounded
outdoors

Never be sure
blame is some joy
and will die
blameless
as joy is

His heart
inching up
to the fire
roars itself
into the sky

Another Orpheus

Hear him waken
parades
bell toll
fire gong

the sea
never failing
exploding earth
carnival

Leave him naked
dazzling
in a room
alone

A first holiday
barely turning
he becomes all
one mirror knows

His last day
a rope
slaps the rafter
laughter below

doors tearing open
a crashing upstairs
love him you
he will never know

ORPHEUS BELOW

A Verse Play in Four Scenes

EDWIN HONIG

CAST

ORPHEUS
EURYDICE
PLUTO
HERMES
CHORUS, *three men and three women*
ANTICHORUS, *three men and three women*

Scene I: On the way to Pluto's kingdom

ORPHEUS. While I live she lives.
She belongs to me.
　　CHORUS. She belongs to no one.
She is with Pluto now,
lord of eternal sleep.
　　ORPHEUS. She belongs to me.
In my breath she lives,
in my heart she sings,
in my eyes she walks
the earth still.

CHORUS. She who was dear to you
is a ghost of memory—
memory, the stage
where the dead walk,
seeming to belong
to someone briefly—
responding to our words
and to our bidding,
greeting the light
that seeks them out
until we who need them—
frightened, yearning,
hungry, shining—slip off,
and memory goes down
the same dark hole with us.
  ORPHEUS. She lives in me. She is not dead.
  CHORUS. Good—then she will live
in you a while.
Your striving now
will some day strangely help you
to relieve the pain of grief.
  ORPHEUS. I cannot abide your words:
empty, careless customary words,
words of no feeling.
  CHORUS. Our words bring you
no personal balm.
Death's custom does not change.
Words comfort the comforter.
The mourner goes uncomforted.
For him the death of one
becomes the death of all.
No one can break his grief
but the cherished one he seeks.

ORPHEUS. Grief? I do not grieve. She lives.
I'll bring her back myself.
CHORUS. How will you do it? Tell us.
ORPHEUS. With my full voice,
with my whole body's voice.
(He begins a high vigorous chant as the scene shifts and the dead appear: the Antichorus, male and female, half reclining as if being embraced by an absent lover. They may move slowly, though not mournfully, in response to his song.)
ORPHEUS. Life is the animal
of the world.
More than all
of us alive,
more than all
of us dead,
each of us
ever born
has only been
one eyeblink
of the animal
of the world.
(Chorus comes to the fore, dividing itself in half, male and female.)
FEMALE CHORUS. The end, the physical end:
the last days, beginning of absence.
Moving back to the last days you see
the tightening and loosening of body.
The body, the pressures, the hundred
delicate maneuverings, the sweat,
the pain, the flash and falling
of spirit, the failing.
Watching the body

fighting the self,
pressing, impressing
its own isolation.
Before the departure,
an absence already begun.

MALE CHORUS. Dogged by the need to rebound,
to measure, explain—some message
to lighten the brain—to tell
why the flagging body,
known to you for so long,
unravels, unhinges,
slips off its life,
to float away in the dark.

FEMALE CHORUS. Now her face finds your eyes
without moving her own;
sees you at last.
but sees you too steadily
to see you at all.
Behind the window of pain
you are left outside.

MALE CHORUS. Between living and dying
the gap slowly widens.

FEMALE CHORUS. Who comes between
to end the deceit?

MALE CHORUS. A dark shaping creature.

FEMALE CHORUS. The sole self moving,
unmoved, irreducible.

MALE CHORUS. Dark creature alone
each of us bears
from birth until death.

FEMALE CHORUS. Unclearly known,
barely acknowledged,
rarely engaged.

CHORUS. The still steady mover
of life's ongoingness.

MALE CHORUS. The end, and you see her
totally changed.
The end after hours
of furious breathing,
the color leaving her face,
a deep blood flush
creeping through her scalp,
the lowered breathing—
the animal rasp.
FEMALE CHORUS. One self-emptying gasp—
and you breathe in her mouth,
her mouth returning it twice
with breaths no longer her own,
before going still.
MALE CHORUS. Her thin loose arms
you try to rub.
They are cold.
FEMALE CHORUS. Her limp wet mouth,
her cheeks cold as meat,
the life pressed out.
MALE CHORUS. There is her head,
composed on the pillow:
your last look turning away
from the open door.
FEMALE CHORUS. No longer herself,
her quiet profile
strangely unchanged,
yet completely another.
MALE CHORUS. As someone asleep
who sleeps so fast
she is no longer herself.
FEMALE CHORUS. The delicate line
of the nose badly stretched,
making it seem almost hooked.
MALE CHORUS. Her wide mouth gaping

flabby, unbreathing.

FEMALE CHORUS. Her yellowing face.

MALE CHORUS. Her life—

FEMALE CHORUS.   —gone out.

MALE CHORUS. Gone out of life.

FEMALE CHORUS. What is the self, the sole self,
barely known, and rarely engaged?

MALE CHORUS. Our only being.
Without it we misunderstand
our love, our despair, our linked
belonging one to another.
Without it we miss knowing
we are who we are.
One life strikes up
in response to another's,
like music.
A singular weight
impresses the stream
of all consciousness
passing now
into forever,
passing forever.
Without it we are nothing—
less than a carrot, a dog.

FEMALE CHORUS. Unburdened when known,
it moves freely,
touching all, of which
it is never a part.

MALE CHORUS. Subsisting in things
it has touched
as if saying, "I am
totally in but not of it."

FEMALE CHORUS. While shaping the form
it is making in order to be.

MALE CHORUS. One form still forming,
unknown till the end,
coming clear briefly.

FEMALE CHORUS. Seen and felt by another,
watching in terror, in love.

MALE CHORUS. As a tide washes in, washes out.

FEMALE CHORUS. As a sigh of spirit achieved.

MALE CHORUS. As a life momentarily fixed,
glimmering clear,
beyond life's urgencies.

FEMALE CHORUS. Finding its shape at last.

MALE CHORUS. Between living and dying,
the gap slowly widens.
Who comes between
to end the deceit?

FEMALE CHORUS. A dark shaping creature.

*(The voice of Orpheus breaks out, repeating the song
"Life is the animal.")*

> Life is the animal
> of the world.
> More than all
> of us alive,
> more than all
> of us dead,
> each of us
> ever born
> has only been
> one eyeblink
> of the animal
> of the world.
> I sing the animal
> of the world.

*(Chorus reassembles, as before, while Antichorus, com-
prising the dead, comes together opposite.)*

ANTICHORUS. Art is his weapon
against immortal death.
CHORUS. Art is his defense
of all life's beauty.
ANTICHORUS. Man wishes to forget
the life he lives.
So much of what he lives
is pain and groveling.
CHORUS. Pain is beauty's animal
and shares with him
all life's changes.
ANTICHORUS. If this were so,
death would not matter,
life would not matter.
Art would have no subject.
CHORUS. There is only life,
the only subject for song.
ANTICHORUS. His song denies the gods
and scorns eternal life.
CHORUS. Eternally his song
honors the life of man.
ANTICHORUS. A blasphemy that men
never will forgive him.
CHORUS. All women need him.
There is the wife he trusts
his art to resurrect.
ANTICHORUS. Through her his art is spent—
his final punishment.
CHORUS. Through her we see all women
rise up to worship him.
ANTICHORUS. Desiring him in body's madness,
as their husband,
their one common god,
they will tear his flesh,
they will break his limbs,

they will crush his manhood,
they will devour him.
>   *(Antichorus divides, male and female, to sing this ballad.)*
> MALE ANTICHORUS.   Let me take you in my arms.
>   Death must make love bloom.
>   I can quiet all your qualms.
>   Death is life's bridegroom.
>   ANTICHORUS. *Over and over the leaves of clover*
> *are plucked, again and again in vain.*
> FEMALE ANTICHORUS. I let you come in one night,
>   worm into my room.
>   Love died in the daily light.
>   Death bulged in my womb.
>   ANTICHORUS. *Over and over the leaves of clover*
> *are plucked, again and again in vain.*
> MALE ANTICHORUS.   I drop you, your taste is gall.
>   Love has had its way.
>   Death dumps clutching lovers all
>   into the light of day.
>   ANTICHORUS. *Over and over the leaves of clover*
> *are plucked, again and again in vain.*
>   *(Enter Orpheus. Seeing Antichorus for the first time, he*
> *approaches them curiously. As he addresses them, each*
> *successively turns away slowly.)*

ORPHEUS. Who are you in that gown with drooping breasts,
like the painted mother of a woman I once knew?
She warned me against seduction of the senses
through music and poetry. Her daughter died.
The mother trailed me till she grew mad.
You're silent now. Why do you turn away?

And this one here, grinning for his pay,
I can remember him. He served me once.
He holds up his two stumps of arms
to show me where the hands were lopped
for stealing something from me once.
Strange, I can't remember what he stole.

Can this be the loose-lipped girl
with hollow eyes, the one who filled
my waking dreams when I was a boy,
who still trembles for her chastity?
She sways as though her great wet eyes
will drag her to the ground. She falls away.

And you—who are you with that face
so empty and immense that only
to approach you makes me want to drown?
Your silence deafens, like the traffic
of a city vanishing in time.
Who or what are you? How you stand your ground!
   (*Antichorus fades away with his last words while Chorus
replaces them at his side.*)
   ORPHEUS. Why are they here?
They steal my breath!
   CHORUS. Your memory wakens them
when you are in despair.
They thrive in misery,
flooding your mind.
   ORPHEUS. I am done with ghosts.
My mind must light her image
till it sings Eurydice awake.
   CHORUS. You will have to go
where death walks endlessly.
He must let you enter freely.
No man has ever gone so far.

ORPHEUS. I am that man—my song will do it!
CHORUS. How? Do you know the way?
ORPHEUS. Through me to her the way lies open.
This is what I know.
*(On upper stage Eurydice appears, loosely veiled, as a kind
of promise. Light pours down on her.)*
ORPHEUS. See now, she lives! She's here!
Where I am she is with me, living!
*(Eurydice makes vague motions, as if to summon him;
then in a burst of menacing and erotic music, she vanishes.)*
CHORUS. We are amazed. You are mortal,
yet you open the way to death,
which only those who die can know
and know once only—on their death.
What is it in you makes you know?
ORPHEUS. I cannot tell you how I know.
Can I tell you how I breathe?
To sing I must know such things
and yet not know them overmuch.
Knowing the way is open, I
must bring her back, or I die.
CHORUS. If she is not already dead,
then she will die. You too may die.
ORPHEUS. You buzz like flies around
a honeypot. Leave me.
CHORUS. Leave you? You keep us here.
Unless you die,
we cannot leave you
nor can we go beyond you.
If you know the way lies free,
go beyond us,
and there, alone,
find the stranger in the dark.
(Chorus fades gradually away from Orpheus.)
ORPHEUS. In the dark I know him.

He is darkness
filling silence
till he owns it all.
A wide opening of nothing
that devours everything.
Fear and joy together
lie down in his arms and die.

I alone am his undoing.
I shall be his undoing.

When he took Eurydice,
all night he breathed against my eyes.
His darkness almost swallowed me.
In his darkness I could drown.
He walled her off from me all night.
All night her cold sweat trickled
down my thighs.
I felt his weight move down on her,
I felt his black tongue move all night,
stoppering her mouth.
All night, all night
my body bruised, my bones were sore.
I turned to her, her breathing stopped.
The dark had swallowed her.

I alone am his undoing.
I shall be his undoing.

I awoke. Eurydice was gone.
I awoke alone. A welling up
of blood rocked my body still.
My sex became a stone.
I saw the door half open—

through the doorway
sunlight bursting.
Sunlight sang me back alive.
Whoever left the door ajar
had let the sunlight in.
Now the song the sunlight sang
is this song I sing.
It will be his undoing.

I alone am his undoing.
I shall be his undoing.

(*In a dazzling light and at the same burst of erotic music
as before, Eurydice reappears, descending, smiling, toward
Orpheus, who remains fixed, concentrated, his back toward
her.*)

BLACKOUT

Scene II: In Pluto's kingdom

PLUTO. I say put him through this thing the hard way.
Let him drag along on wounded legs,
his guts torn open like a crippled dog,
all the way downhill on his belly.
HERMES. Come on. He's a magician: Orpheus,
poet-musician, darling of the gods.
For him it has to be a special lark.
Sweating's only for heavyweights like Hercules.
PLUTO. I don't see it. If he doesn't suffer,
what good is it to him—being in hell?
Tear him apart is what the thing must do.
HERMES. You're fond of bloody messes. I'm not.
You're talking of religion. Me, I love
the living; apparently you don't or can't.

PLUTO. Somebody's got to draw the line between
the living and the dead . . .

HERMES.   Why? Why not
let souls spill over so the living can
come down and get to know the place they fear
or bring the dead back for a holiday?

PLUTO. Blasphemer! Only gods are glorious
and powerful forever; man himself
is muck, up in a flash, out in a fizzle.
Only a god comes down here and gets back.

HERMES. It's true, the gods delight to see men wriggle
like worms; it makes them feel superior.
Why else would you have let the poet come
down here to take his wife back? Do you care?
Were you showing off? What if he makes it?

PLUTO. Makes it? Isn't that your job to see
he doesn't?

HERMES. No, it's yours. You're boss. You asked him.

PLUTO. His music got me. A weak moment. I still
can't say just why I promised.—To stop his music!
Unbearable! It made me want to die!

HERMES. That's amusing—so awfully human! You're
undead—
I mean, Lord of the Dead, a god, eternal!
Just think, you've got to live with you forever!

PLUTO. It gets a little fierce here—all the silence.
Then music filled my ears. I went weak,
I guess, and so my head nodded to him.
"Come take her, yes, but only stop the music!"
Silence again. I roared, "But if you look
at her before you reach the light—she's gone!"

HERMES. Wanting to be alive—meaning undead.
When gods get bored they play at being human,
and right away the pleasure's too much for them.
They call it weakness and impose the law.
You own the place and keep the score, so tell me,

landlord, isn't that what hell's about?

PLUTO. Also, you must make sure that he stays put.
You're responsible for him.

HERMES.   But not for you!

PLUTO. You've got to understand the way things are.
I can't allow these madmen, poets, prophets,
to hop down here and back. It breaks the law,
and it could kill morale, starting them all
to dreaming the old dream—to live forever!
The dead exceed the living now something
like two million to one. Think of the mischief
if some little man like Orpheus should start
hauling them all back again to earth!
Give him an inch and there's no stopping him.

HERMES. And who was it, tell me, gave him that inch?

PLUTO. But I admit a little weakness. I'm only—

HERMES. Immortal, yes. Also a statistician,
a bigot, prude, and lowest lowdown member
of the establishment. Like me you're cursed
enough with single-mindedness. At least
I know how huge one human wish can be.
I can perambulate among the spheres.

PLUTO. Then you'll take care of Orpheus for me?

HERMES. I like wild music and the passions. Listen.

(Music bursts through, and Orpheus descends; Pluto
immediately retreats.)

NO CURTAIN OR BLACKOUT

49

Scene III: The same as Scene II

(As Orpheus slowly descends, his way ahead is marked by a sharp narrow blue light. This gradually gives just enough illumination to bring the Chorus and the Antichorus out of the darkness on opposite sides. Stage center the figure of Hermes emerges, waiting. Orpheus stops when he becomes aware of Hermes.)

HERMES. Welcome to Death's kingdom.

ORPHEUS. *(beginning to approach)*
I do not know you.

HERMES. I am Hermes. I come to guide you.

ORPHEUS. *(confronting him)*
I do not need you.

HERMES. Perhaps not. We'll see.

ORPHEUS. *(passing him)*
I do not want you.
(The blue light dims and goes out. Orpheus stops.)

HERMES. Have you been here before?
You insist you know the way.
Consider, this is not earth,
no halfway place, but hell,
where everything is total.
Darkness is pitch darkness.
Death is stony death.

ORPHEUS. Until this point my way was lit.
A blue light led me like a hand.

HERMES. Yes, human consciousness
deserves to be displayed here.
You're living and full-blooded,
a man carrying full tilt a mind,
a soul, and an immense idea.
These need to be lit up.
But you reach beyond a certain point,

50

and, as you see, that point is here.
Here's where Pluto reigns,
fanatic keeper of the dead.
He rules beyond the limit
where life contains itself no more,
where breath and all the faculties
no longer function. Except in certain
special cases, they usually stop.
That's why I've been sent to you,
to help you on the way from here,
and lead you living to your dream.
    ORPHEUS. I do not need your guidance.
I go the way I am
through darkness and through death.
My song will give me breath.
    *(A female member of the Antichorus rushes to embrace
Orpheus excitedly. Again the erotic music. Orpheus looks
closely, as if she might be Eurydice, then turns away. Hermes
has not noticed the interruption. The blue light comes on
and sharpens with the first word of Hermes' reply.)*
    HERMES. Then go ahead, I'll follow—
leading from behind.
    ORPHEUS. My mouth wells up with song,
yet song won't lead me to her.
The breath in silence leaving
and re-entering my body
yearns toward her body,
making a song of nothing,
making breath itself enough.
I am a stone against a tree
aching to be that tree—
to grow, to shed its leaves
and sleep, yet never dream
what was or what will be.

In sleep I am that girl I seek,
cradled in our bodies' love.
Come, love, take away my breath!
 *(Another female member of the Antichorus breaks loose,
as before, and with a cry embraces Orpheus. The same music
and wordless action follow.)*
  CHORUS. You are the harvest of the earth beginning.
Think that alone, in yearning and in growing,
and the fruit drops from the tree.

You are the hard ground over deep earth's longings.
Be that alone, in sleep's long burrowings,
till the fruit drops from the tree.

You are the seed through frozen winter burning
with root love, and with the worm still turning
when the fruit drops from the tree.
  ANTICHORUS. We taste the ripened pips,
and sweetness bursts our lips.
We crunch the crisp thighbone,
our teeth glinting like stone.
  CHORUS. What lives must feed on what's alive.
What's dead feeds on itself.
If the dead cannot live again,
the still-living may not die.
Yet they do—both things occur.
The dead live frozen in the mind.
The living, though still standing, die
feeding on grief, the dead belief,
bloated with wild memory,
in past beauty die.
  ANTICHORUS. Spend yourself, give self away
to death, then think no more, and die.
   (echo) and die.
Living for you is past, praise death.
Becoming what you dread, so die.

      (echo) so die.
The tree you were became a stone,
believing in stone, though standing, dead.
      (echo) standing dead.
   (Erotic music mounts, a crashing light, and Orpheus falls;
Eurydice appears at once behind him, glowing.)
   HERMES. Orpheus, stand up, she is here.
You must lead her back.
This is what you came to do.
   (Orpheus rises, lightly supported by Hermes, who faces
him sideways, where he can see Orpheus and also look toward,
though not at, Eurydice.)
Poised behind you now,
she lights up emptiness
like the Venus star.
She is all you thought,
answering your thought,
telling how she came here.
   (A silence, then an increasing, heaving, rolling sound—like
waves of death.)
   EURYDICE. I rode the waves to shore
where I was deposited.
Then I saw the tide withdraw,
the beating roar subside.
I was alone again as when,
ripped from my mother's blood,
I fell into the breathing world.
Why do I stand waiting again
to learn which way to go,
wondering how to go?
Does the body live or die?
   ORPHEUS. You are all voices filling my mind
when it pleases and is pleased,
yet not one voice I yearn to hear.
   CHORUS. She is your nature mirrored in a gift.

She is your passion spent and hovering.
She returns herself faithfully to you.
   ORPHEUS. She returns faithfully,
but not herself to me.
Her voice is all voices
cherished by memory,
but not one of them
comes alive to me.
Although I may not see her,
her speech denies her presence.
She is far away, though near.
   HERMES. You must not question what
is different or the same.
In your way you have found her,
now lead her away.
   ORPHEUS. What Eurydice is this,
speaking to what I was,
not to what I am?
   CHORUS. In asking for her
you asked for what
had died in you.
   ANTICHORUS. Now die with her.
This is what you sought.
This is why you came.
   CHORUS. Leave her now.
You no longer
need to have her back.
   HERMES. You came for her.
Now lead her back.
   ORPHEUS. First she must speak
in her own voice,
the voice I know as hers,
a voice I can recall.
Until I hear that voice
I sense her presence only,
not her life, behind me.

54

I did not come to find
a faithful loving ghost.
I came to bring her back,
my fully living wife.
    HERMES. Until you speak to her,
she has no present life.
Until you lead her back,
her voice is in the past,
remaining all it was
when you saw her last.
    ORPHEUS. I do not want her ghost.
    HERMES. Then win her back to life.
Move, and she follows you.
Speak, and she will answer.
    *(Orpheus moves and starts back, ascending, the blue light
pointing the way ahead. Behind him, slightly to the left, is
Hermes, and last, directly behind, is Eurydice.)*
    ORPHEUS. Eurydice, I feel your soundless steps,
your breathless mouth, behind me.
    EURYDICE. Yes, Orpheus. I follow where you go.
    ORPHEUS. I lead you back to life.
    EURYDICE. Yes, Orpheus, I know.
    ORPHEUS. Do you want to live?
    EURYDICE. I do not know how to want.
    ORPHEUS. Do not be afraid.
I will teach you how to want
and how to live again.
    EURYDICE. If I had fear, it would be for you.
If I had love, it would be for you.
I do not know what feelings are.
I have no sense of pain or sorrow.
Only some memory of knowledge.
I know you called me and I follow.
    ORPHEUS. First and last learn joy again
for all things living in their being.

I bring them back—the taste
of fruit, the leap of animals,
bird-glide and fish-turn,
where water is deep fire,
where all the air embraces earth.
I praise man and the creatures,
I praise the trees, the plants,
I praise the stones,
I praise the farthest star
pulsing in the eye.
Now the night listening
to the word is shriveling.
    EURYDICE. Won't the day shrivel too?
Won't the day, listening
to the word, shrivel back
into the night already
shriveling into day?
    ORPHEUS. As I listen, a silence dies
and the word rises, rising
out of my hand to speak.
Where is the silence that lives
on this world, listening?
What listens beyond me?
Eurydice, come follow me!
    (As they continue to move, the blue light intensifies.)
    EURYDICE. I follow you, Orpheus.
    ORPHEUS. *(half turning)*
Eurydice, I know your voice,
it is your own voice I hear again.
    HERMES. Orpheus, take care; turn like that
again, and she is lost to you.
    (Shadows begin to appear, moving.)
    ORPHEUS. Eurydice, I know the way
is past these shadows
moving here beyond us.

They are and they are not,
and yet move endlessly.

EURYDICE. It is the moving of other people
thinking beyond you,
creating and destroying,
doing the people-things.
You cannot even watch them.
They walk through you.
To them you are invisible.
To them only they move,
they who without knowing it
are invisible too.

ORPHEUS. Tomorrow we will appear.
Tomorrow for the first time
there will be the sequence
of the living and the dead united.
Together there will be
only the instant meeting
of thought with thought.
Living and dead will be one.
Nothingness will disappear.

EURYDICE. Yesterday I remember I was yours.

ORPHEUS. So you will be again tomorrow
when we rise from this cold night.

EURYDICE. Will I remember what I was today
tomorrow? Will this sense
of being nothing, which is all
I am now, except the voice you give me,
return to cover up my mouth?

ORPHEUS. Eurydice, the voice you say
I give you is yours, not mine.
You will know that in your blood
before you face the light again.

CHORUS. Her blood is sluggish, scarcely moves.
Her limbs follow his but only

as if wired to his words.
He knows this well but is too fond and
of the remembered flesh she gave his words
to go back to doubting her again.

ORPHEUS. The light falters. I cannot see.
(Blue light dims.)
HERMES. It is still your light, remember—
your own, to bring you and return.

CHORUS. Her new fatigue has wearied him.
Look how his arms fall to his sides.
His drooping head searches the ground
for signs. Sink! say his halted feet.

ORPHEUS. *(straining not to turn)*
Eurydice, my wife,
take on my present life!

EURYDICE. My body yearns to be dissolved.
Now held together only by
your wish, it washes on my mind
and tugs it down like crumbled stone.
Believe me, Orpheus, each fiber in me
cries out to my blood to stop,
be still, become invisible!

*(Female Antichorus moves in a group to block Orpheus,
in attitudes half appealing and half menacing, as if he were
their glittering prey. Orpheus turns away from them.)*

ORPHEUS. I must free her of the past.
Eurydice, my wife,
I give you all my breath!

*(Turning back completely, he lunges past Hermes to
embrace Eurydice, and comes away holding her shroudlike
garment, empty, in his hand.)*

EURYDICE's VOICE. Orpheus, rejoice, for I am dead.
I no longer need to rest in you.
Voiceless now I am myself,

the emptiness held in your hand
no longer burdens memory.
Orpheus, you are free to be
the voice you sought in me.
Thank you for my life, my death.
   (*As Orpheus begins to tear her garment to shreds, female
Antichorus surrounds him, singing.*)
   FEMALE ANTICHORUS. Life is the animal
                             of the world.
                             More than all
                             of us dead,
                             each of us
                             ever born
                             has only been
                             one eyeblink
                             of the animal
                             of the world.

   (*Orpheus manages to break loose from them, going
upward, where the light pours forth, but they follow intently,
already holding in their hands parts of his dress: a sandal, his
belt, and so forth.*)

                        BLACKOUT

                Scene IV: The same as Scene II

   PLUTO. You think he escaped?
   HERMES.   You mean she didn't.
   PLUTO. Who ever said she would?
   HERMES.   You pretend,
now that it's over, you weren't scared
she would—with your permission too.
   PLUTO. I swear it won't happen again.
   HERMES. I don't know. Mortals have a way

of coming back for more once they
have tasted the impossible.

    PLUTO. Ah, just plain greediness. What else?

    HERMES. No, it's passion leading them astray,
but passion brings on something more
abiding: a growing itch to transcend
empty time and circumstance.

    PLUTO. Ach, there you go again, blaspheming.
Only the gods transcend. Everyone
knows that. Men are flies. They live
and die between a yawn and sleep.
They just don't have the grip we do.

    HERMES. Pluto, tell me, what brought him here?
—Yes, Orpheus. To this hell hole?

    PLUTO. Some insane notion that he was
better than the gods, I guess.

    HERMES. Oh, use your head. The impulsion's
got to be a lot more personal
to drive a man down here. Think again.

    PLUTO. All right: the gods themselves, his music.
You said he was their darling. Well,
it was a trick to put me down.

    HERMES. Come, come, Pluto. We all know you're
tone-deaf. Besides, since when have men
needed the gods except as means
toward a special end? You think
he'd go through hell just to put down
a minor deity like you?
For God's sake, try to see it his way!

    PLUTO. What are you getting at? I think
I see your meaning—a woman! You mean
the woman, Eurydice? For her sake?
The maddest thing I ever heard!
Sure, men have got to procreate—
that's how they keep alive enough

to not mind dying. But with a dead one?
Aren't there enough live women
up there he could jump on without
killing himself to get a dead one?

HERMES. All right, you're getting warm—if I
dare use the word about you. Hasn't
it ever struck you that love and sex
are man's way to transcend himself?

PLUTO. You must be joking. Love and sex?
For bulls and horses! *(laughing)* No? Yes!

HERMES. Yes, laugh yourself sick over it.
Most gods do. They have no choice.
Thinking yourself immortal you find
the urge to love is just the fault
that makes man mortal, like an animal,
or else the sadly childish way
he has of finding comfort in the dark.
But there's more to it than that.

PLUTO. *(still laughing)*
More to it than what? What else
but lovely sex? Or sex and love!

HERMES. It's the end of the gods. Orpheus
will ring the curtain on the gods
because even if he failed to take
his wife back from the dead, he has
opened the way to conquer death.
With love. With art. With life itself.
He's shown men what's inside them, what they
can be through what they feel and think,
despite the gods. Men following him
displace the gods, become eternal.

PLUTO. *(stops laughing, though still shaking)*
Displace the gods, will he? And where
d'ye think your little man is now?

(Displaying long swatches of Orpheus' torn-out hair,

with bloody skin still attached.)

HERMES. Pluto, where did that come from?

PLUTO. The women chasing him. They did
a job on him—tore him apart!
You know, and some who missed out on
his feel while he was still alive,
they got to eating him—his rump,
his face, his big male thing, even
his eyes and nails taste good to them.

HERMES. Just sound and fury, a new religion!
Still, how disagreeable!
Devour him, then puff his image
up, and raise him to the skies!
They'll forget he was a man who used
his brain to undermine the static
hell of dying gods. Now women
make *him* a god—an antihuman
floating abstract thing, an iceberg
stuck way up in some heaven they
must go down on their knees to worship,
guiltily, of course, since they've thrown
their brains away to do it. Sinful,
agh! Do you suppose men love death
more than they love their own lives?

PLUTO. Well, he's dead anyway. You know from what?
(laughing) What did you call it? Lovely sex?
Oh, love and sex! Well, what does that
lead to, tell me, if not to death?

*(Hermes turns away; Pluto goes down on all fours,
laughing uncontrollably.)*

BLACKOUT .

62